CW00847980

Letters to

JESUS
AND MY GOD

Letters to
JESUS
AND MY GOD

CONNIE EARLY

XULON PRESS

Xulon Press
2301 Lucien Way #415
Maitland, FL 32751
407.339.4217
www.xulonpress.com

© 2023 by Connie Early

All rights reserved solely by the author. The author guarantees all
contents are original and do not infringe upon the legal rights of any
other person or work. No part of this book may be reproduced in any
form without the permission of the author.

Due to the changing nature of the Internet, if there are any web
addresses, links, or URLs included in this manuscript, these may have
been altered and may no longer be accessible. The views and opinions
shared in this book belong solely to the author and do not necessarily
reflect those of the publisher. The publisher therefore disclaims
responsibility for the views or opinions expressed within the work.

Paperback ISBN-13: 978-1-66286-723-1

I would like to dedicate this book to my son David.
Thank you son.

Tell me Jesus

Help me understand

Why you love me so

This lowly soul

Not deserving of you

I am nothing special

I can never repay you

For what you have done for me

Yet you're always there

Each and every day

and I can only imagine

The love you have for me

But I do know

I will love you

Forever

If not for the blood of Jesus

Where would I be

So down so lost

Never to be found

But Jesus died for me

and now I see

The love He has for me

He chose the cross

His love I have

and now my Jesus

I will live for you

Oh my soul
Who do we need
We need the One
Who is true
The one who loves us
Will never leave us
The One who will make us new
He shed His blood
Upon that cross
To show His love
To save us all

When I wake in the morning

Who do I see

I see You Jesus

In my heart

In my mind

All around me

In the sky

In the birds

In the flowers

And in the trees

In the night

In the moon and stars

My Jesus my Lord

You are everywhere

Before the sun comes up
And the birds start to chirp
I listen to the silence
And hear your voice
My heart reaches out for you
I long to draw you near
My love for you consumes me
I cannot hold it in
As I go about my day
I take you with me
Holding your hand
Walking in the light
I love you

As I walk along the path

That seems to go on and on

I wonder how far it goes and if there is an end

I wonder what I will find when I reach the end

In a way I am anxious

In a way I am nervous

But I keep on going

Because I know

At the end

I will find you Jesus

Sometimes I wonder

If my faith is enough

Will Jesus see me through

Will He be there

When I am so down

Will He help me climb out

Of the darkness

I know He will

if I believe

He will keep His promises

He will never let us down

His love will never cease

We are His children

He is forever

He is Love

My heart is so full
My soul cries out
I can hardly contain
What I feel inside
It seems like a hand
Is squeezing me tight
And will not let me go
It wants to hold me
Oh so close
Til I beg for release
But then I realize
That what I feel
Is what I need
It's you Jesus

$\mathcal{I}$ see your arms
Reaching for me
I see your face
Shining down on me
I feel your Spirit
Dwelling within me
I feel Your love
Surrounding me
I am so grateful
and blessed and happy
That I am your child
A child of God

$\mathcal{I}$ see you so high above
Looking down upon your children
Wanting us to come back to you
We have gone so far astray
What has happened to us
We don't seem to care
We have lost our way
Somewhere back when
Before we knew
Who you truly are
Help us Lord help us see
That we really do need you

Some days I wake

To a day so dreary

I wonder where is the sun

But as the day

Brings forth it's light

Then I smile at last

Because I know

That you are there

Wanting to walk with me

I am so eager

I reach for your hand

and together we will travel

along the path

you have set for me

$\mathcal{I}$ will follow you

Wherever you may lead

Whatever you may want

From me

You are the One I love

You are the One I give

My life to

There is no other

Who could ever compare

To you

You are my everything

Oh my Jesus

I long for you

My heart is so full

I can not contain

These feelings inside

But how do I let them go

I want to sing

I want to shout

Your name Oh Jesus

I love you I need you

Please do not let me go

You are all I want

You are all I need

With you I am safe forever

Bless the Lord

Oh my soul

For all that He has done

Give Him thanks

and all our love

and all our obedience

He deserves it

He is Holy

He is our Father

and He loves us

He gives to us

Our heart's desire

Pray for us Oh Lord

We need You more

Then ever now

So many of us

who do not see

who do not know

You like we should

Your love for us

Is so amazing

How could we not know

How You gave Your life

To save us

Your children

Sometimes I am up

Sometimes I am down

Sometimes I do not know

which way to go

My head is whirling

I feel like I am spinning

around and around

How can I stop

Please reach out your hand

and hold on tight

and then I will know

That I am safe

In your arms

In the morning

When I wake

I reach out my arms to you

If only I could touch you

How happy I would be

I long to be with you

But while I am here on earth

I will carry you in my heart

I will walk with you

all the day long

 I will love you

and I will praise you

I will wait for you

To come for me

Sometimes I wonder

If I am doing it right

These roads I am taking

My soul is saying

Take me higher

Way up to the stars

I want to climb

To be with you

To not be alone anymore

But now I don't have to

Because you said

"Follow Me"

and I did

Now I have your love

and you have mine

Oh Jesus what would I do

If you were not in my life

I would be in a world

I do not want

A world empty and void

So many things

Want to pull me down

I do not like the dark

I need the light

and that's where you are

You fill me with love

I open my eyes

and you are there

My life is now complete

You called my name

You said I am yours

Oh how happy I am

I have someone

I can depend on

Someone to lean on

Someone who cares

Who will lead me

When I stumble

Will lift me up

If I fall

You are my lifeline

I am so blessed

You are my all

Father God look down on me

Look into my heart

See the love I have for you

It makes me shiver

It makes me shake

All that is inside me

You know who I am

You know what I want

You know that it is you

You called me

 and I answered

Here I am I am yours

$\mathcal{I}$ reach my hands

Up to the sky

Hoping to get close to You

My need my dream

Is all about You

I want to know you better

My heart cries out

I need you so

I feel so lost without you

Please let me know what I can do

You are my all and all

My life is yours

I give it to you

Because I love you

$\mathcal{I}$ see you Jesus
I know you are there
I see your face
Smiling at me
wanting me to know
That you are waiting
Silently patiently
and when you are ready
You will come for me

$\mathcal{I}$ want to tell

The world about you

I want to tell them

Who you are

I want to tell them

What you've done for me

How my life has changed

I want to tell them

Of your goodness

and how much love you have

For all of us your children

There is no end

Every morning fresh and new

I have your forgiveness

I get to start a whole new day

To give my love to you

I worship you

You are my everything

There is nothing else I want

Nothing else I need

I want to see your face

I want to hold your hand

I want to walk with you

All the way to Heaven

$\mathcal{I}$ see you there

I run to you

To be held in your arms

I feel so safe

I do not fear

It's where I want to be

They call to me

To come and play

But when I look it's dark

Then I turn back to you

and you smile at me

and hold me tight

You are my desire

You are my hope

You are the One

My heart yearns for

My soul cries out

I need You so

Please take my hand

Pull me close to You

And then you whisper

In my ear

You are safe now my child

Sometimes I turn around

and I feel so lost

I see nothing around me

I reach out

To find something to hold

and there is nothing there

But then I hear a voice

A small still voice

Calling to me

Come my child I am here

I reach out my hand

and you touch me

Jesus my lifeline

What a friend

We have in Jesus

It's a song I heard long ago

I never knew

Just what it meant

Until I needed you

I cried out

It hurt so much

and you touched me

You said "I am here"

You said "lean into me"

and I did

and I know

That You are my friend

$\mathcal{I}$ lift my eyes

To the One up above

My prayers and love abound

I raise my hands

and reach up to You

I see You smiling down

You tell me how

You will walk with me

Every single day

You promised You

Would hold on to me

and never let me go

I feel so warm

I feel at peace

Because You are there

You said when we are troubled

To bring our cares to you

You said when we are hurting

To lay them at your feet

You said that you feel our pain

 and will take them all to heart

and then you will give us

What we really need

You will give us comfort

and will always walk us through it

You will draw us close to you

and say "It's ok I am here."

Oh my Lord

Today I will sing

Songs of praise to You

Knowing I make You smile

Also makes me smile

I want to sing

I want to dance

I want to run

I want to float

All that is in my heart

Is yours

Father God

You gave me Your Son

He was a part of You

But You loved me so much

You were willing to give Him up

I know that I can never

Make up for all You give me

No matter what I do

You will never leave me

No matter how bad I am

You will never stop loving me

When I cry You wipe away my tears

When I call out to you

You are there

Jesus You gave Your life for me

You loved me so much

You willingly let yourself

be beaten, mocked and

nailed to that cross.

My heart hurts so when I think of it.

What can I give You in return?

I can only love You

with everything in me

and live as You lived.

For now I will hold You in

my heart until you come back

to take me home to Heaven.

CPSIA information can be obtained
at www.ICGtesting.com
Printed in the USA
BVHW032315130223
658422BV00004B/34

9 781662 867231